EARLY LEARNING
For three- to five-year-

Jenny's Surprise

Story by Pie Corbett
Activities by David Bell, Pie Corbett
Geoff Leyland and Mick Seller

Illustrations by Diann Timms

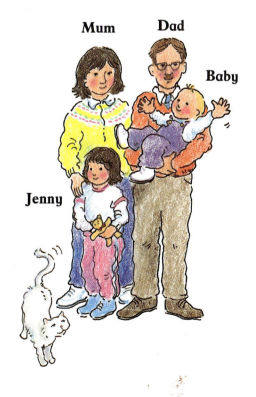

It was raining.
Jenny was bored.
There was nothing to do.

What do you do when it rains?
Could you draw a rainy day picture?
Put into your picture some of the things you like to do on a rainy day.

'Dad, can I have a story?'
'In a minute,' muttered Dad.

Dad has told Jenny to wait a minute.
What could you do in a minute?
Could you walk round your house in a minute?
If you have a clock with a second hand, you could watch a minute go by.
Can you guess when a minute has gone by?

'Mum, can I watch television?'
'In a while,' said Mum.

Have you ever talked to someone on the telephone?

The next time it is someone's birthday, you could ask Mum or Dad to help you to ring them up to say 'Happy Birthday' as well as sending them a card.

These are two ways of sending messages. Can you see any other ways of sending messages in the picture?

'Dad, can I go to Gran's?'
'Maybe later,' said Dad.

Look at all the bubbles in the picture.

Ask Mum or Dad if you can blow some bubbles.

Blow the biggest bubble that you can.
Now blow the smallest.

Can you catch a bubble?
If you can, look at the colours in it.
Can you see through it?
Don't hold it too close to your eyes.

'Mum, can Yasmin come round?'
'We'll see,' said Mum.

Everyone except Jenny seems busy.
Do you have any jobs to do at home?

Who would you ask around and what would you do?

What do you think is going to happen?

Yasmin is a good friend of Jenny's.
Do you have a good friend?
What are your other friends like?

'Dad, give me a piggy back.'
'Not now, Jenny,' said Dad.

Look at all the clothes coming out of the washing machine.

Some belong to Mum, some belong to Dad, some belong to Jenny and some belong to Baby.

How would you sort them out?

Would you sort them by colour or would you sort them by size?

Can you think of any other ways of sorting the clothes?

Jenny felt fed up.

Look at the newspaper on the floor.

Can you see the advert for the circus?
Ask someone to help you read it.

What day of the week does the circus begin?

How much does it cost for a child to see the circus?
How much does it cost for an adult?

'Come on, Mum, we could go to the circus.'

'If you're good, dear,' said Mum.

Draw a picture of a clown, and ask Mum or Dad to help you turn it into a circus poster.

Don't forget to put on the dates, what it costs to go and where the circus will take place.

Do you think that Mum will take Jenny to the circus?

'Dad, let's dress up as clowns.'
'Mmmm,' mumbled Dad.

Do you know why Dad is putting cream on Baby's bottom?

Ask your mum or dad to help you find out.
Put a piece of kitchen towel on a tray.
Put some baby cream on one part of it.
Pour a little water on the part with the cream and then on the part of the towel without cream.

What happens to the drops of water?

How would this stop Baby's bottom from getting sore?

'Baby - let's play custard pies.'
But Baby was busy.

How many red bricks can you see?

The blue bricks are stacked on top of each other.
Point to them and count them.

Now look for five green bricks.
Can you find them all?

'Dad, you juggle with the oranges,
Mum, you can be ring-master,
Baby can bang the drum and
I'll jump through a hoop.'

Nobody listened.

Have you ever seen a juggler?
Can you catch a ball?
Who is the best thrower in your family?
Put a box on the floor.
Take turns to throw a small ball into it.
You could make up some rules for the game
to find out who the best thrower is.

It stopped raining.
Jenny went outside.

Does anyone want to play with Jenny?
Why don't they want to play?
Do you think she is pleased that it has stopped raining?
What would you do now?
What can you see in the picture that Jenny could play with?

She watched the raindrops drip.

Wait for a rainy day. When it has stopped raining, put on your mac and wellingtons like Jenny and go outside with your Mum or Dad.

Can you see any droplets dripping off the leaves?
Find the biggest droplet you can.
Talk together about where you would find the most droplets.

'Come on in, Jenny,' called Mum.
'I've got a surprise for you.'

Do you love surprises?
Can you guess sometimes what the surprise is going to be?

It would be a nice surprise for someone if they received a letter from you. You could send a drawing and a letter to, say, your gran or grandad, to tell them about what you've been doing.

You could ask someone to write down what you want to say to them.

If you write a surprise letter to someone, maybe they will write a surprise letter back!

Ask a grown-up to help you draw, colour and cut out some oranges like the ones in the picture.

Can you make a circle with the oranges?
Can you make a square?
Can you make an oblong?

Cut out some more oranges.
Can you still make the circle, square and oblong?

Activity Notes

Pages 2-3 Young children need to have plenty of early experience of using different materials such as pencil, crayon, chalk, paint, Plasticine, play dough, glue, paper, card or fabric. They will need some help and guidance with jigsaws and other puzzles, plus plenty of praise. Finished work should be pinned up for all to see. These early activities help develop hand control which is needed for handwriting.

Pages 4-5 Young children find the concept of time difficult to grasp. They need to have the opportunity to do things for fixed periods, eg, 30 seconds or one minute. This allows them to develop an understanding of units of time and to use appropriate language to describe the passage of time.

Pages 6-7 There are many ways of passing on information. Look through books and magazines to find examples of signs and signals and talk about what they mean. Draw some pictures to show the main events of a typical day together. Decide who you would like to pass on this information to. Perhaps you could post one to yourselves.

Pages 8-9 This activity encourages children to look closely at bubbles and to build a greater understanding of a familiar object.
You could go further by asking, 'Can you make a square bubble or a long bubble?', 'Does the bubble always burst when it touches something?'.

Pages 10-11 Thinking about what might happen next is an important part of learning to read. You might also ask why the adults are not paying any attention to Jenny. How do you think she feels? These sorts of questions may direct your child to reading beyond the words and appreciating what is going on in the story.

Pages 12-13 Sorting allows children to develop an understanding of similarity and differences, important concepts before children can begin to count. It also helps them to classify objects according to different criteria such as colour or size.

Pages 14-15 Opportunities for maths are all around and although young children might not be able to read the language of posters, timetables or signs, they should be encouraged to look for numbers or prices which give mathematical information. In this way, maths is seen as practical and relevant to day-to-day life.

Pages 16-17 This activity could lead into your child making humorous posters, eg, 'Lost! One Grey Sock' or 'For Sale! One Younger Brother'. When looking at posters, signs or labels, show your child the key words as you read them.

Pages 18-19 The cream helps to keep Baby's bottom dry so that it doesn't get sore. Talk about the way we keep ourselves dry when it's raining. Together, make a collage of pictures cut from old magazines to show wet- and dry-weather clothing. Talk about waterproof clothing.

Pages 20-21 Sorting by colour helps children to count individual items. Early counting is best done by asking children to point to, touch or physically move items that are being counted.

Pages 22-23 Having formed rules for the game, keep a score of successes out of ten. Now change hands - will the score be as good this time? Have a guess and then find out. Continue this process. Test a prediction by repeating the game with one eye closed. Try standing further away or using a smaller box.

Pages 24-25 These questions are intended to help your child consider how Jenny feels. Talking about how characters feel in a story, what has happened and what might happen are all important elements in becoming a reader and deepening understanding of a story. What may be obvious to you may not be to your child.

Pages 26-27 Careful and patient observation is an important skill to learn as well as being a rewarding experience in itself. While you are outside, find other things which you can look at together. Ask questions in order to encourage close observation. For example, look at a tree trunk: 'What colour is it?', 'Is it all brown?', 'Is the bark rough or smooth?'.

Pages 28-29 Sending and receiving letters is a great boost to both reading and writing because it is an activity with a real purpose. If your child has lots to say, take over the writing; in this way, more can be written. Or, let your child write in their own writing and write underneath it in yours. Make letter writing and receiving fun.

Pages 30-31 Young children soon recognise and name two-dimensional shapes. Encourage this and introduce more shape names progressively. Additionally, children should be encouraged to describe the different attributes of shapes, eg number of faces, number of sides, etc.

32